BATS

NANCY J. SHAW

CREATIVE PAPERBACKS

BAT

In ancient times people in Europe were afraid of bats and thought they were evil.

Vampire bat

Bats have been flying on Earth for more than 50 million years. These amazing animals can be found nearly everywhere on Earth, but many people have never seen a bat up close.

Published by Creative Paperbacks
123 South Broad Street, Mankato, Minnesota 56001
Creative Paperbacks is an imprint of The Creative Company

Designed by Stephanie Blumenthal
Production Design by Melinda Belter

Photographs by: Frederick Atwood, Earth Images, FPG International, Fletcher
and Baylis, GeoIMAGERY, Dwight Kuhn, Joe McDonald, Peter Arnold, Inc.,
Rainbow, Rob and Ann Simpson, and Tom Stack & Associates

ISBN 0-89812-318-6
Library of Congress Number 00-101552

First Paperback Edition

2 4 6 8 9 7 5 3 1

BATS AS MAMMALS

A bat is a **mammal**. Next to rodents (mice, squirrels, and rabbits), bats make up the largest group of mammals. Like cats, dogs, humans, and other mammals, bats have furry bodies, they are **warm-blooded**, give live birth to their young, and their mothers nurse them on milk.

Unlike all other mammals, however, bats are the only ones that can truly fly!

Mexican free-tailed bat

BAT ART

The Mayan culture embraces bats in their folklore and art. Mayan ruins in Central and South America have been found decorated with bat designs.

BAT

WORD

In China the bat symbol, "fu," is used to decorate fabric, pottery, and jewelry. The word for happiness is also pronounced "fu," just like bat.

Because bats are active at night, or **nocturnal**, we may not know a lot about them. They are gentle, shy, and helpful creatures. They are social animals, and most kinds live together in large groups, or colonies.

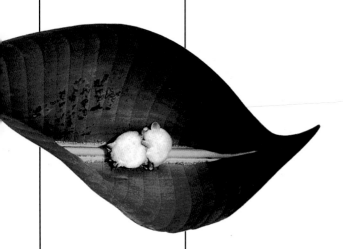

Above, tent bats; right, white-lined sac-winged bats

Also, bats are very clean, and they spend much of their time grooming themselves and each other as they rest upside-down in their homes, called roosts.

Below, Virginia big-eared bat resting on a little brown bat

BAT

A bat's grip is so strong that some are found still hanging when they are dead.

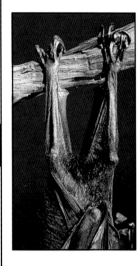

Above, feet of a flying fox; center, bat wings are filled with veins

BAT BODIES

Bat wings are not covered with feathers like birds; rather, they are actually two thin layers of skin stretched between the long fingers of small hands. Bats can move their fingers as we humans move ours, and they are able to change the shape of their wings with each movement of their long fingers. This allows them to make complicated maneuvers in flight that birds would find difficult.

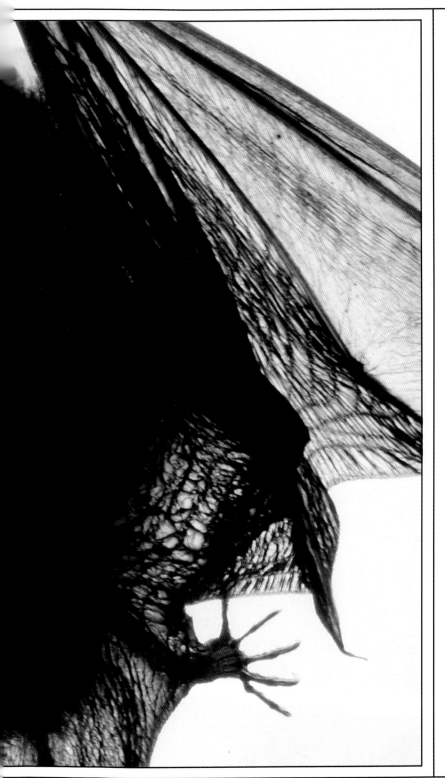

Bats can swoop, dive, hover, turn sharply, and catch and hold their **prey** with their wings, which are really hands.

A bat has five pointed claws, or toes, on each of its two feet. In most species, the skin of the bat's wing stretches from the fingers to the feet, and even to the tail (if the bat has a tail).

9

Above, bats have fingers on the forewing

BAT

BUMBLEBEE

The smallest bat in the world, the Kitti's hog-nosed bat of Thailand, is very small—only about the size of a bumblebee.

Hoary bat

When not in flight, bats hang upside-down, gripping hold tightly with their clawed toes. Bats hang from roofs, cave ceilings, or high branches to avoid animals that hunt them for food. Some of these predators are cats, snakes, weasels, raccoons, and foxes. Even while in flight, bats must be alert to predators such as hawks and owls.

BAT

BREAKFAST

A single North American bat can easily devour up to 600 mosquitoes in just one hour.

Left, California leaf-nosed bat; below, neotropical fruit bat

Bats come in many different sizes and colors, and each species has its own special look. The face of a bat—its ears, eyes, nose, and mouth—indicates to which species it belongs.

BAT

FACT

There are so many different kinds of bats in the tropics that bat species often outnumber all other mammal species combined.

Above, Philippine bat; top right, spectacled flying fox; bottom right, Egyptian fruit bat

BAT VARIETIES

There are nearly 1,000 kinds of bats on Earth. Many of these species are rare and have become **endangered** by humans destroying their **habitats**. Bats help people in many ways, but humans are the most dangerous enemy of bats.

Bats belong to the scientific order of animals called Chiroptera, which means "hand-wing" in Latin. About 200 species of bats belong to the suborder Megachiroptera, which means "big hand-wing." We call them **megabats**.

Many of these large tropical bats are also called "fruit bats" because they eat fruit. There are no megabats in North America. Most of the smaller bats, the remaining 800 species, belong to the suborder Microchiroptera, which means "little hand-wing." These **microbats** are the kinds you will see flying around your yard if you live in the United States or in any **temperate** climate, where it is cold for only part of the year.

13

Horseshoe bats have large ears and elaborate "nose leaves" that they use for echolocation.

Little brown bat

BAT

Tourists visit the Carlsbad Caverns of New Mexico just to see thousands of Mexican free-tailed bats leaving the caves every evening.

Above, Malaysian fruit bat; right, big brown bat

Some of the most commonly seen microbats in North America are the big brown bat, with a wingspan of about 12 inches (30 cm), and the smaller little brown bat, with a wingspan of about eight inches (20 cm).

The fisherman bat of Mexico and South America is one of only three kinds of bats that eat fish.

Hoary bat

The hoary bat is the largest bat in North America. This bat's wings may stretch 16 inches (41 cm), and its reddish-brown fur is flecked with white, giving it a frosty look. It is one of the most colorful and handsome bats living in North America.

BAT

GIANT

Flying foxes are the gentle giants of the bat world. Some adults have a wingspan of nearly six feet (1.8 m).

Right, flying fox; far right, leaf-nosed bat in flight

Red bats are also common in North and South America and are among the fastest flying bats. They can reach speeds of more than 40 miles (65 km) per hour. Most other bats fly at speeds between 10 and 20 miles (16–32 km) per hour, depending on the species.

BAT

BARE

Most bats are furry, but the naked bat of Borneo and the Philippines has no fur at all.

Tent-making fruit bats

BAT HABITATS

Bats live everywhere except the Arctic and Antarctic regions (where it's too cold for bats to survive) and a few remote, or distant, islands and deserts. While 42 species of bats live in the United States and Canada, most of the world's bat species live in the **tropics**, where there is an abundance of food and warmth all year long.

There are 14 species of bats in the United Kingdom, and a national law protects them all from human interference.

Left, a sacred bat cave in Bali, Indonesia; above, brown bat

D epending on the species, bats choose different roosts. Many bats live in dark, sheltered places such as caves, and in attics of barns, churches, and houses. A single cave can be the home for millions of bats.

While species of temperate bats must migrate to warmer places or hibernate to survive cold temperatures, bats that live in very warm climates neither migrate nor hibernate and often make their homes in trees. Leaf-nosed bats bite holes down the center of a banana leaf, which then folds down over them like a tent, protecting them from the rain and hot sun.

Right and far right, flying foxes

Some people make houses for bats called "bat boxes" and hang them in their yards to attract bats. Having a small colony of bats is a wonderful way to keep down the number of insects in your yard.

BAT
BUTTERFLY

Tiny butterfly bats of Africa have spots on their wings and hover in the air like butterflies; they are active during the day rather than at night.

BAT

*The two-inch (5 cm)
long ears of the long-
eared bat are almost
as big as its body.
They are so big that
the bat curls them up
when he roosts.*

*Above, vampire bat;
right, young Malaysian
fruit bats*

BAT PARENTS

When a female bat is ready to give birth, she will leave the colony to set up a **nursery**. There she, along with many other pregnant females, will give birth and care for their tiny babies, called kids or pups.

The young of most microbat species are born in 40 to 60 days. This period varies in megabat species. Vampire bats take the longest—eight months.

Most bats have just one baby at a time, but red bats of North America have two to four babies at once, and the mother even carries them all with her as she flies.

Philippine bat

The kid is born live, feet first, and totally helpless. It drops into the safety of its mother's wings and clings tightly to her furry body with its feet. While most microbats are born hairless with their eyes closed, megabats are born with thick fur and open eyes.

BAT
BLANKET

When a horseshoe bat roosts, it wraps its wings all around itself so that only its tiny feet stick out.

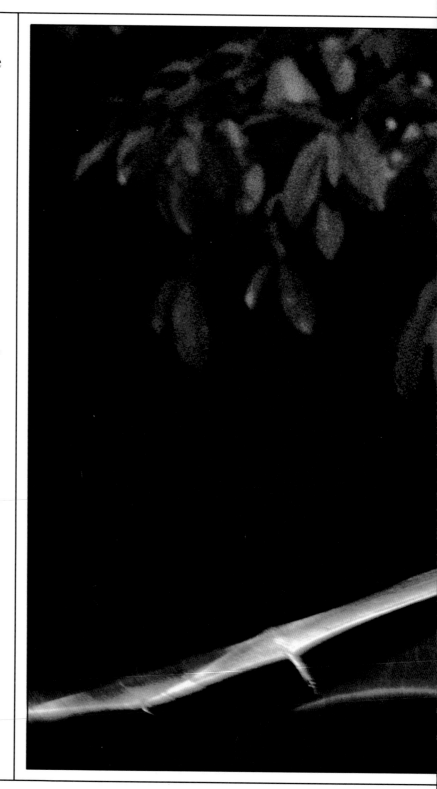

When the mothers are out hunting for food, the kids hang closely together for warmth. If a kid loses its grip, it will fall to the ground—most likely to its death. When the mother bat returns, she will search out and nurse only her own kid among the many hungry babies.

Right, Malaysian fruit bat with baby clinging underneath

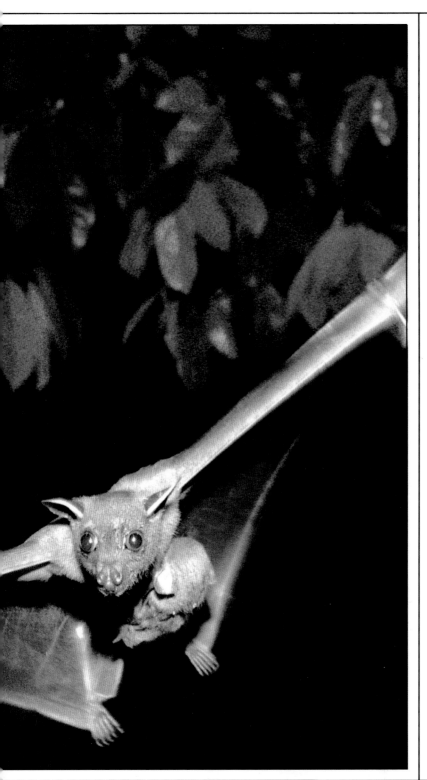

Baby bats grow quickly, and some species learn to fly by three weeks of age. But before they leave their nursery roost, they practice flying with their mothers. Sometimes a kid will cling to its mother's body as she flies from place to place in search of food.

BAT
BIZARRE

The hammer-headed fruit bat of Africa has a face resembling a horse, and the males croak like a frog to attract females.

Above, hammer-headed bats have no **sonar**

BAT
TAIL

Most bats' tails are built into the wing, but the mouse-tailed bat's tail hangs out behind its wing like a mouse's tail.

Right, flying foxes; far right, leaf-nosed bat

HOW BATS HUNT

Finally, the young kids are ready to leave the nursery. They will learn to hunt their prey using **echolocation**. As bats fly they make **ultrasonic** squeaking and clicking sounds that bounce off objects and travel back to their ears like echoes.

These echoes not only tell the bat the exact location of its prey, but also the size and shape of the prey. This amazing ability allows bats to judge where their prey is and how fast it is moving. It also keeps bats from flying into things like trees or buildings in the dark.

BAT

GHOST

Ghost bats of Australia are named for their nearly white fur. They eat birds, frogs, and small mammals—including other bats.

Above, ghost bat, or "false vampire" bat; center, bats are sleek, silent hunters

28

WHAT BATS EAT

Since bats are nocturnal creatures, they search for food during the night and spend the day grooming, resting, and sleeping.

Different species of bats eat different kinds of food. The megabats of Africa and Asia, commonly called "fruit bats," feed only on flower nectar and fruits. Other bats eat frogs, lizards, fish, or even birds. But most of the world's bats eat small insects, including flies, moths, and mosquitoes. In fact, 70 percent of all bat species are **insectivores**. In just one night, a bat can eat half of its own body weight in insects.

Probably the most feared and famous of all bats, the vampire bat, feeds on the blood of animals.

But don't fear—vampire bats, which make up a very small group of the world's bats, rarely bite humans. Vampire bats can run quickly across the ground on their strong legs and climb up the back of sleeping cows or horses. They use their large upper teeth to bite the animals, then lap up the blood with their tongues. Bat **saliva** thins blood, allowing it to flow freely without clogging as the bat drinks from its host.

BAT
SIPPER

Many bats drink water by skimming their tongues on the surface of a pond or lake as they fly over, and some lap the dew from flowers and leaves.

BAT
STICKY

The sucker-footed bat of South America hangs head-up by its thumbs, instead of upside-down by its toes, as do most other bats. Little suction cups on its wrists help it cling to a leaf as it roosts.

BAT

F A C T

Bats seem to be silent when they fly, but really they are almost always making the high-pitched sounds they use for echolocation.

Top right, New Guinea fruit bat; bottom right, Seminole bat; far right, spectacled flying fox

WE NEED BATS

Besides helping to control the world's insect population, bats are major seed spreaders and **pollinators** of many plant species. The success of the great baobab tree of Africa and the giant flowering cactus of Mexico is totally dependent on the bats that come at night to drink nectar from the flowers of these plants.

Bat droppings, called guano, are an excellent fertilizer and are harvested by people in countries such as Mexico and Thailand.

W e need bats and bats need us. Many people are trying to help bats by teaching others about the importance of bats in nature. Scientists continue to study bats, special bat preservation groups have been formed, and the U.S. government is making new laws to protect bats and their homes for future generations. Everyone agrees that we have much more to learn about these fascinating creatures of the night.

Glossary

Certain animals such as bats and dolphins emit high-pitched squeaks and clicks to determine the direction and distance of objects. This is called **echolocation**.

Endangered animals are threatened with becoming so few in number that their kind will die out completely and disappear from the earth.

Habitats are the places where animals or plants naturally live and grow.

Animals that survive on a diet consisting only of insects are called **insectivores**.

A **mammal** is any kind of animal that gives live birth, feeds its young with milk from the mother's body, and whose skin is covered with hair or fur.

Any bats belonging to the suborder Megachiroptera are **megabats**; they are the larger of the bat species.

Any bats belonging to the suborder Microchiroptera are **microbats**; they are the smaller of the bat species.

Animals are **nocturnal** if they rest or sleep during the day and are active and hunt at night.

A **nursery** is a special area where newborn and young babies are kept and cared for.

Pollinators transfer the pollen from one plant to another; pollination is needed for plants to reproduce.

Prey is the term used for any animal that becomes a meal for another animal.

Sonar is used to hear and make ultrasonic sounds.

A **temperate** climate has changing weather that is neither too hot nor too cold.

The southern **tropics** are the southernmost areas of our planet. The sun shines very brightly there and the weather is very hot.

The human ear cannot hear **ultrasonic** sounds, but certain animals such as bats and dolphins can hear them—and make them as well.

A **warm-blooded** animal has a normally constant and warm body temperature regardless of the temperature of the environment around it.